ALMOST TWINS

by

Anna Moates and Anna Penland
Foreword by Liz Plachta

Published by Happy Self Publishing
www.happyselfpublishing.com

HAPPY
SELF PUBLISHING

DEDICATION

We dedicate this book to our amazing family members: Ken, Valerie, Brittany, Ashley, and Christopher Moates, and Mike, Rebecca, and Caroline Penland. We are so grateful that they have given us the opportunities to grow up in a loving home and have been so supportive on our Auburn University journey.

We further dedicate this book to the Auburn University EAGLES Program. This program, for those with intellectual disabilities, has changed both of our lives for the better and it has brought us this lifelong friendship - and a student family as well. We will always owe our fondest memories throughout college and the years beyond to the EAGLES Program. It has taught us much about how people are unique. We are all different, but yet similar in so many wonderful ways. We are excited to watch the EAGLES Program continue to grow, thrive, and transform lives.

FOREWORD

I am honored to be writing this foreword for Almost Twins written by Anna Moates and Anna Penland. I am the Executive Director of Ruby's Rainbow, a nonprofit that grants scholarships to people with Down syndrome for college while showing the world just how amazing and capable they are! Anna Moates is one of our Rockin' Recipients and continues to break down barriers and stereotypes for people with disabilities. She was the first student with Down syndrome to be accepted to Auburn University since it was founded in 1856, and we are proud to have been able to help her go for her dreams of higher education and independence. I cannot wait to see what she continues to accomplish in her lifetime! My most important job is being a mom to my beautiful daughters, Ella Mae and Ruby. Ruby just happens to be rockin' that extra chromosome just like Anna! Seeing Anna have beautiful friendships and be included in her community and beyond gets me so excited for my own daughter's future! This book is a perfect example of how friendship and inclusion work both ways and benefit EVERYONE!

Keep on rockin' it Anna! We are so proud of you!

Liz Plachta
Ruby's Rainbow
Co-Founder, Executive Director
Proud mama to Ruby

Hi - My name is Anna!
I have a HUGE
imagination.

I was born with an extra
chromosome, so I have
something called
Down syndrome.

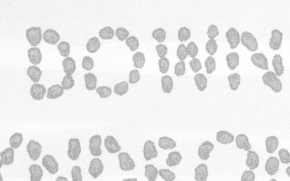

DOWN SYNDROME

It is not a disease. You cannot catch it from someone else!

Some people are just born that way. It just makes things a little harder for them, but it also makes them really awesome.

Sometimes, I get really creative, and I imagine having a twin sister.

In real life, some people have a hard time understanding exactly what it is that I am trying to say, but this twin understands EVERYTHING I say. I never have to repeat myself and she lets me sing as loud as I want to!

It makes me feel really happy to imagine this twin sister and feel so understood because I do have some differences. But I recently found something even better...

"She met me! My name is Anna too. We have the same name and love a lot of the same things. So, it is like we are real life twins... almost." We don't live in the same state or have the same parents, but when we met and had so much in common, the rest was twin history.

"Alright, alright- back to me! Today is VERY special because Anna and I have big plans ahead!"

We both love to sleep...a lot. So today, we decide to sleep in super late, then Anna comes and picks me up for lunch at our favorite restaurant.

I know what to order, my favorite of course. Pizza.

But sometimes my words come out fuzzy instead of clear.

No worries! My almost twin reminds me to slow down my words or use my phone app that can read out my thoughts.

Pizza

Also, she encourages me to repeat what I want to say as many times as I need to for the waitress.

As we wait for our food to arrive, we talk about our plans for the rest of the day. We need to get decorations, tell everyone where to meet and set everything up. We're doing our favorite thing - planning a surprise party for our friend's birthday.

First, we go to the store to buy decorations. My almost twin is very forgetful, so it's a good thing I have a great memory! I pull out the shopping list: balloons, streamers, and food... lots of food.

After we get all of our supplies, we listen to our favorite music as we head back to my house. We laugh because we both are singing as loud as we can and turn it into a singing competition, as usual.

"I will text all of our friends to arrive at 6 o'clock, so we have enough time to get ready," my twin says.

We put on our favorite, pinkest outfits and help each other look our very best, because we will be taking lots of surprise party pictures.

We organize the party supplies, string up the colorful streamers, and blow up the balloons making sure that every inch of the house is decorated. We set out the pizza, napkins, plates, and cups.

We even make a photo booth for our guests. I help Anna hang it because she can't reach the top of the wall on her own. We laugh and cheer because the room looks magical now. Almost twin teamwork rules the day!

As our friends arrive, I tell everyone to be quiet and hide, so they don't give away the birthday surprise. Anna and I tell them all to jump up on the count of three when our friend enters the room.

ONE, TWO, THREE

We did it! We hug the biggest hug ever, knowing we planned a great party filled with dancing, giggles, pictures, food, and storytelling. Our friends celebrate us for planning the best surprise party of the year.

Anna thanks me for helping her with the things she couldn't do without me - hanging the banner, remembering the small details, and just making her happy with my smile.

I thank her for driving me around town for our errands, for reminding me that I am amazing just as I am, and for always making me smile too.

As we clean up after the party, we discuss our plans for tomorrow. "Maybe we could cook dinner or do a movie night tomorrow... I am a little tired from tonight," I say.

Anna gets a twinkle in her eye, "I was thinking the exact same thing!"

As she drops me off back home, we wave goodbye. We both feel so much love just knowing how we both help and enjoy being with each other every single day.

I get excited for tomorrow, because every day is an adventure when you have a twin... well.. an almost twin.

DID YOU KNOW

Down syndrome is a genetic disorder that can cause heart defects, breathing difficulties, muscle weakness, developmental delay, hearing and speech problems, and other health complications.

People with Down syndrome have an extra chromosome that makes their mouths a little smaller, tongue a little bigger, and muscles a little weaker.

Bright smile

Need to belong

strong body

Pretty eyes

A loving heart

Hugging arms

FUN FACTS

1 in 700 babies are born with Down syndrome each year.

 Many colleges have programs that give students with Down syndrome the chance to go to school and make friends like the Annas. visit rubysrainbow.org to see a schoarship program for those with Down syndrome to attend college. See the foreword written about this book, by their founder!

There are many famous models that have Down syndrome now, showing the world how beautiful differences can be.

 Someone with Down syndrome completed an Ironman Triathlon for the first time in November 2020

People with Down syndrome can get a driver's license and drive just like everyone else, if they can pass the test, just like Anna Moates did!

ABOUT THE AUTHORS

ANNA MOATES, a native of Smithville, GA, is the youngest of four children and always assumed she would follow in their footsteps and attend college. She has long aspired to be a trailblazer for others with disabilities and is currently a senior at Auburn University (EAGLES Program) as Auburn's first ever student with Down syndrome. Her favorite on-campus activities include performing with the Auburn University Singers and attending Phi Mu sorority events. In her spare time, she pursues her passions of reading, music, church, horses, writing songs (one of which has been copyrighted!), and hanging out with friends. Anna is so excited for you to get to know her and read about her sweet friendship with her "almost twin" Anna Penland.

ANNA PENLAND is a recent Auburn University graduate and First Grade teacher in Greenville, South Carolina. She has always had a passion for education and has spent much of her time volunteering for the EAGLES Program at Auburn University, where she and her almost twin first met. She has received various leadership and volunteer awards in her community. Anna loves to cook, travel, sing, and be with friends or family. She is so excited to have this opportunity to show people what it is like having a best friend with a disability. It is important to notice that we all have strengths and weaknesses, and it is wonderful to have someone in her life that cheers her on through all of it.

www.thealmosttwins.com

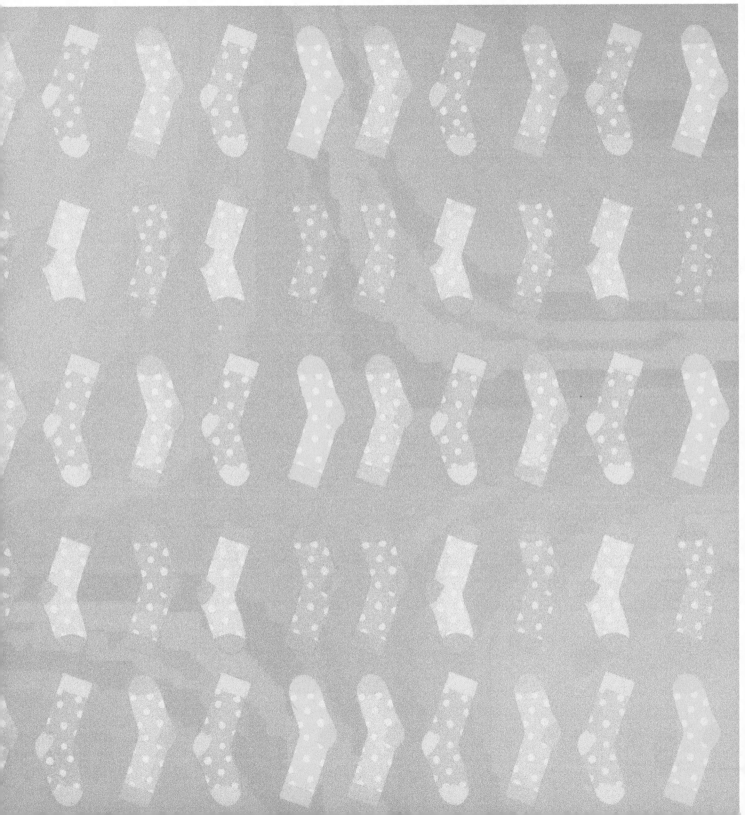

CPSIA information can be obtained
at www.ICGtesting.com
Printed in the USA
BVHW020216020921
PP12579600001B/26